Bredele

vom Elsass
from Alsace

Rezepte / recipes
Nicole BURCKEL
Bernadette HECKMANN
et les Boulangers d'Alsace

Fotos / Photos

Frédérique CLÉMENT

I. D. L'Édition

INHALTSÜBERSICHT

Anisbredele	4
Anna Biskuits	6
Basler Brunsli	8
Butterbredele	10
Cookies	12
Coquins oder Spitzbube	14
Corinthentaler	16
Florentins	18
Glasierte Nuss Steine	20
Gefüllte Tricorne	22
Haselnusshalbmonde	24
Hefebrezel	26
Husarenknöpfe	28
Lebkuchenzüngle	30
Leckerli	32
Liebestaler	34
Makronen-Sandplätzchen mit Himbeermarmelade	36
Männele	38
Mini Linzer	40
Schokoladenmakronen	42
Schokoladenrosette	44
Schokoladenzüngle	46
Schwowebredele	48
Schweizer Sandgebäck	50
Springerle	52
Spritzbredele	54
Süße Brezeln	56
Vanille-Kipferle	58
Weihnachtssterne mit Mandelbaiser (Meringe)	60
Zitronen- oder Orangennuggets	62

CONTENTS

Aniseed Biscuits 4

Anna Biscuits 6

Chocolate Spiced Biscuits 8

Butter Biscuits 10

Cookies 12

Little Rascals 15

Currant Coins 16

Florentines 19

Glazed Nutty Rocks 20

Stuffed Tricorns 23

Hazelnut Crescents 24

Barm Pretzels 27

Hussar Buttons 28

Spiced Cat's Tongues 31

Yummies 32

Love Coins 34

Macaroon Sponge Cakes with Raspberry Jam 37

Little Men 39

Mini Linzer Biscuits 41

Chocolate Macaroons 43

Chocolate Rosettes 44

Chocolate Cat Tongues 46

Schwobebredele 48

Swiss Sponge Cakes 51

Little Jumpers or Little Knights 53

Christmas Biscuits 54

Sweet Pretzels 56

Vanilla Crescents 58

Christmas Stars with Almond Meringue 61

Lemon or Orange Nuggets 63

Anisbredele

Trocknen: 12 Stunden • **Backen:** 10-15 Minuten • **Temperatur:** 150°

Zutaten • 250 g Zucker • 3 ganze Eier • 250 g gesiebtes Mehl • 10 g Aniskörnle

Zubereitung

• Eier und Zucker 20 Minuten schlagen. • Anis und Mehl dazu geben. • Teig in den Spritzbeutel mit glattem Einsatz geben und auf Backpapier oder Silikonfolie in runde Formen spritzen. • 12 Stunden an einem zugfreien Ort trocknen lassen. • Die Oberfläche sollte danach matt und trocken aussehen. • Backofen auf 150° vorheizen. • 10-15 Minuten backen. Die Bredele müssen weiß bleiben.

Aniseed Biscuits

Drying out time: 12 hours • **Baking time:** 10-15 minutes • **Temperature:** 150°C

Ingredients • 250 g sugar • 3 whole eggs • 250 g sifted flour • 10 g aniseed

Preparation

• Mix the eggs and sugar together for 20 minutes. • Add in the aniseed and flour. • Spoon the dough into a piping bag with a smooth nozzle, and pipe into circular shapes on a baking or silicone sheet. • Leave to dry for 12 hours in a cool place. • Afterwards, the surface should look matt and dry. • Preheat the oven to 150°C. • Bake for 10-15 minutes. The biscuits should still be pale.

Anna Biskuits

Backzeit: *10 Minuten* • **Temperatur:** *170°*

Zutaten • *350 g gesiebtes Mehl* • *250 g temperierte Butter* • *125 g gehakte und gegrillte Haselnüsse* • *100 g Puderzucker* • *1 Päckchen Vanillezucker* • *1 Prise Salz*

Zum Bestreichen • *1/2 Glas Milch* • *10 g Kakao* • *100 g Puderzucker*

Zubereitung

• Alle Zutaten (außer die zum Bestreichen) zu einer homogenen Masse kneten. Aus dem Teig eine Wurst von ca. 4 cm Durchmesser rollen. • Mit der Milch bestreichen und die Wurst in der Kakao-Puderzuckermischung wälzen. • Die Wurst 2-3 Stunden im Kühlen ruhen lassen. • Danach von der Wurst 5 mm dicke Scheiben abschneiden und kleine Würstchen (länglich wie Brotform) formen. • Die Biskuits auf Backpapier oder Silikonfolie legen und mit dem Puderzucker bestreichen. • 10 Minuten bei 170° backen.

Anna Biscuits

Baking time: *10 minutes* • **Temperature:** *170°C*

Ingredients • *350 g sifted flour* • *250 g softened butter* • *125 g chopped and grilled hazelnuts* • *100 g icing sugar* • *1 packet vanilla sugar* • *1 pinch salt*

Coating • *1/2 glass milk* • *10 g cocoa* • *100 g icing sugar*

Preparation

• Knead all the ingredients (apart from those for the coating) into a smooth dough. Roll into a sausage about 4 cm thick. • Brush the sausage with milk and roll it in the cocoa-icing sugar mixture. • Leave to rest for 2-3 hours in a cool place. • Cut the sausage into 5 mm thick slices and roll these into smaller sausages (lengthwise, shaped like bread). • Place the biscuits on baking paper or silicone sheet and sprinkle with the icing sugar. • Bake for 10 minutes at 170°C.

Basler Brunsli

Backzeit: *2-3 Minuten* • **Temperatur:** *230°*

Zutaten • *250 g Puderzucker* • *250 g gemahlene Mandeln* • *40 g Kakao* • *75 g Eiweiß von 2 großen Eiern* • *1/2 Kaffeelöffel Zimt*

Dekoration • *Zucker*

Zubereitung

• Alle Zutaten zu einer homogenen Masse kneten. • 2-3 Stunden im Kühlen ruhen lassen. • Zucker auf die Arbeitsplatte streuen und den Teig darauf 1 cm dick ausrollen. • Teig mit beliebigen Ausstechern ausstechen und auf Backpapier oder Silikonfolie legen. • Backofen auf 230° vorheizen. • Backen: 2-3 Minuten.

Chocolate Spiced Biscuits

Baking time: *2-3 minutes* • **Temperature:** *230°C*

Ingredients • *250 g icing sugar* • *250 g ground almonds* • *40 g cocoa* • *75 g egg whites from 2 large eggs* • *1/4 teaspoon cinnamon*

Decoration • *Sugar*

Preparation

• Knead all the ingredients together into a smooth dough. • Leave to rest for 2-3 hours in a cool place. • Sprinkle sugar over the work surface and roll the dough out to a thickness of around 1 cm. • Cut out the dough using your preferred pastry cutter and lay the pastries on the baking paper or silicone sheet. • Preheat the oven to 230°C. • Bake for 2-3 minutes.

Butterbredele

Ruhezeit: *2 Stunden •* ***Backzeit:*** *10-15 Minuten •* ***Temperatur:*** *180°*

Zutaten *• 250 g gesiebtes Mehl • 1 Kaffelöffel Backpulver • 125 g temperierte Butter • 125 g Zucker • 3 Eigelb • 1 Päckchen Vanillezucker • 1 Prise Salz*

Zum Bestreichen *• 1 Eigelb*

Zubereitung

• Temperierte Butter, Zucker, Vanillezucker, Salz, Eigelb und gesiebtes Mehl und Backpulver gut mischen und zwischen den Händen zu einem Sandteig reiben. • Teig zu einer Kugel formen und in einer Frischhaltefolie 2 Stunden im Kühlen ruhen lassen. • Backofen auf 180° vorheizen. • Teig 4 mm dick ausrollen und mit Weihnachtsförmchen ausstechen. • Bredele auf Backpapier oder Silikonfolie legen und mit einem Pinsel mit Eigelb bestreichen. • Trocknen lassen und ein zweites Mal bestreichen. • 10-15 Minuten backen bei 180°.

Butter Biscuits

Resting time: *2 hours •* ***Baking time:*** *10-15 minutes •* ***Temperature:*** *180°C*

Ingredients *• 250 g sifted flour • 1/2 teaspoon baking powder • 125 g softened butter • 125 g sugar • 3 egg yolks • 1 packet vanilla sugar • 1 pinch of salt*

To glaze *• 1 egg yolk*

Preparation

• Mix together the softened butter, sugar, vanilla sugar, salt, egg yolks, sifted flour and baking powder well. • Rub this mixture together with your fingers until it resembles fine breadcrumbs. • Shape the dough into a ball, cover in cling film and leave to rest for 2 hours in a cool place. • Preheat the oven to 180°C. • Roll out the dough until it is 4 mm thick and cut out the biscuits using Christmas cutters. • Lay the biscuits on baking paper or silicone sheet and brush the tops with the egg yolk. Leave to dry and then brush over once more. • Bake for 10-15 minutes at 180°C.

Cookies

Backzeit: *10-15 Minuten* • *Temperatur:* *180°-190°*

Zutaten • *120 g Butter* • *80 g Zucker* • *120 g brauner Zucker* • *1 Päckchen Vanillezucker* • *2 Eier* • *1 Eigelb* • *300 g gesiebtes Mehl* • *100 g gemahlene Haselnüsse* • *6 g Backpulver* • *1 Kaffelölffel Zimt* • *350 g Schokoladensplitter*

Zubereitung

• Mehl, Backpulver und Zimt sieben. Gemahlene Haselnüsse dazugeben. • Butte, Zucker, brauner Zucker und Vanillezucker mit dem Mixer gut verrühren. Nach und nach die Eier und das Eigelb darunter mischen. • Mehlmischung vorsichtig unter die Masse heben. • Zuletzt die Schokoladensplitter darunterheben. • Teig zu einer 3-4 cm Durchmesser dicken Wurst rollen. • 1 cm dicke Scheiben schneiden. • Cookies auf Backpapier oder Silikonfolie legen. • Backofen auf 180°-190° vorheizen. 10-15 Minuten backen.

Cookies

Baking time: *10-15 minutes* • *Temperature:* *180°-190°C*

Ingredients • *120 g butter* • *80 g sugar* • *120 g brown sugar* • *1 packet vanilla sugar* • *2 eggs* • *1 egg yolk* • *300 g sifted flour* • *100 g ground hazelnuts* • *6 g baking powder* • *1/2 teaspoon cinnamon* • *350 g chocolate chips*

Preparation

• Sift the flour, baking powder and cinnamon together into a bowl. Mix in the ground hazelnuts. • Using a mixer, whisk together the butter, sugar, brown sugar and vanilla sugar. Slowly add in the eggs and egg yolk, bit by bit. • Gently fold in the flour mixture. • Finally, stir in the chocolate chips. • Roll the dough into a 3-4 cm thick sausage. • Cut into 1 cm thick slices. • Lay the cookies out on baking paper or silicone sheet. • Preheat the oven to 180°-190°C. Bake for 10-15 minutes.

Coquins oder Spitzbube

Ruhen: 1 Stunde • **Backen:** 10-15 Minuten • **Temperatur:** 180°

Zutaten • 120 g Zucker • 1 Prise Salz • 1 Ei • 220 g Mehl • 25 g gemahlene Mandeln • 125 g temperierte Butter • 1 Kaffeelöffel Zimt • 1 Päckchen Vanillezucker

Garnitur • 150 g rote Früchtemarmelade • 50 g Puderzucker

Zubereitung

• Ei, Zucker, Vanillezucker und Salz schaumig schlagen. • Mehl und gemahlene Mandeln auf die Masse geben und mit den Fingerspitzen leicht zu einem Teig darunter heben. • Butter in kleinen Stückchen dazu geben und das Ganze zu einem Teig kneten. • Teig zu einer Kugel formen und in eine Frischhaltefolie wickeln. Eine Stunde im Kühlen ruhen lassen. • Backofen auf 150° vorheizen. • Teig auswalzen und mit einem Ausstecher (5 cm Durchmesser) ausstechen. • Die Hälfte der Plätzchen mit einem Fingerhut oder Apfelausstecher in der Mitte ausstechen. • Plätzchen auf ein Backpapier oder Silikonfolie legen. 10-15 Minuten backen. • Nach dem backen eine nussgroße Menge Marmelade in die Mitte der Plätzchen geben und die ausgestochenen Plätzchen darauf setzen. • Die Conquins oder Spitzbuben mit Puderzucker bestreuen.

Little Rascals

Resting time: 1 hour • **Baking time:** 10-15 minutes • **Temperature:** 180°C

Ingredients • 120 g sugar • 1 pinch salt • 1 egg • 220 g flour • 25 g ground almonds • 125 g softened butter • 1/2 teaspoon cinnamon • 1 packet vanilla sugar

Coating • 150 g jam from any red fruit • 50 g icing sugar

Preparation

• Whisk together the egg, sugar, vanilla sugar and salt until creamy. • Stir in the flour and ground almonds, then using your fingertips rub together until the mixture forms a batter. • Add in the butter piece by piece and the knead everything together to form a smooth dough. • Shape the dough into a ball, cover in cling film and leave to rest for 1 hour in a cool place. • Preheat the oven to 150°C. • Roll out the dough and cut the biscuits out using a 5 cm diameter cutter. • Cut out the centres of half of the pieces with a thimble or apple corer for the lids. • Place all the pieces on the baking paper or silicone sheet. Bake for 10-15 minutes. • After baking, place a nut-sized mound of jam in the middle of the whole biscuits and cover with the cut out lids. • Dust the „Little Rascals" with icing sugar.

Corinthentaler

Backen: 10-15 Minuten • **Temperatur:** 180°

Zutaten • 200 g temperierte Butter • 200 g Zucker • 1 Päckchen Vanillezucker • 3 Eier • 500 g Mehl • 200 g in Rum eingeweichte Corinthen

Glasur • 30 ml Schnaps • 120 g Puderzucker

Zubereitung

• Am Abend zuvor die Corinthen in Rum einlegen. • Backofen auf 180° vorheizen. • Butter, Zucker, Vanillezucker schaumig rühren. • Nach und nach die Eier dazu geben. • Das Mehl gesiebt und zuletzt die Corinthen dazu geben. • Mit 2 Kaffeelöffeln Häufchen auf das Backpapier oder Silikonfolie geben. • 10-15 Min. backen.

Glasur
• Puderzucker mit Schnaps verrühren und nach dem Backen die Taler damit bestreichen.

Currant Coins

Baking time: 10-15 minutes • **Temperature:** 180°C

Ingredients • 200 g softened butter • 200 g sugar • 1 packet vanilla sugar • 3 eggs • 500 g flour • 200 g rum-soaked currants

Glaze • 30 ml Schnapps • 120 g icing sugar

Preparation

• Cover the currants with rum and leave to soak overnight. • Preheat the oven to 180°C. • Whisk together the butter, sugar and vanilla until creamy. • Slowly add in the egg, bit by bit. • Fold in the sifted flour and, finally, stir in the currants. • Using 2 teaspoons, form small mounds on baking paper or silicone sheet. • Bake for 10-15 minutes.

Glaze
• Stir the Schnapps into the icing sugar and brush over the biscuits after baking.

Florentins

Backzeit: 10 Minuten • **Temperatur:** 180°

Zutaten • 75 g süße Sahne • 75 g Zucker • 25 g Honig • 30 g Mehl • 50 g in Würfel geschnittene kandierte Orangenschale • 25 g in kleine Stückchen geschnittene kandierte Kirschen • 60 g gehobelte Mandeln • 100 g schwarze Blockschokolade

Zubereitung

Backofen auf 180° vorheizen. • Silikon- oder Backform mit Törtchenausbuchtungen auf Blech oder Backgitter legen. • Sahne, Milch und Honig in einem Kochtopf unter ständigem Rühren zum Sieden bringen bis sich kleine Bläschen bilden. • Ca. 5 Minuten bei 118° kochen lassen. • Falls Sie keinen Thermometer haben, kann man die Masse kontrollieren, indem man einen Tropfen ins kalte Wasser gibt. • Es bildet sich dann eine weiche knetbare Masse. • Den Topf vom Herd nehmen. • Kandierte Früchte, Mehl und Mandelsplitter gut darunter mischen. • Einen Kaffeeklöffel dieser Masse in jedes Förmchen geben. • Ungefähr 10 Minuten backen bis die Florentiner eine schöne blonde Bräune haben. • In dieser Zeit Schokolade im Wasserbad zergehen lassen. • Nach dem Backen die Florentiner abkühlen lassen bevor man sie auf ein Gitter legt. • Die Backform waschen und trocknen und wieder auf das Backgitter legen. • 1 Kaffelöffel flüssige Schokolade in jedes Förmchen geben. • Das Backgitter auf die Arbeitsplatte leicht klopfen, sodass die Schokolade sich schön verteilt. • Jetzt die Florentiner auf die noch weiche Schokolade setzen und im Kühlschrank 2 Stunden erkalten lassen.

Ratschlag • Die Florentiner nicht länger als 10 Minuten backen, selbst wenn man das Gefühl hat, dass sie noch weich sind. • Beim Abkühlen werden sie fest.

Florentines

Baking time: 10 minutes • **Temperature:** 180°C

Ingredients • 75 g cream • 75 g sugar • 25 g honey • 30 g flour • 50 g chopped candied orange peel • 25 g candied cherries • 60 g flaked almonds • 100 g dark cooking chocolate

Preparation

Preheat the oven to 180°C. • Place a fluted tart tin or silicone mould on a baking tray or mesh. • Mix the cream, milk and honey together in a saucepan and constantly stirring, heat until simmering. Leave to cook for about 5 minutes at around 118°C. • If you don't have a thermometer, you can check the mixture by dropping a little into cold water. It should form a soft, kneadable dough. • Remove the saucepan from the stove. Thoroughly mix in the candied fruit, flour and flaked almonds. • Place ½ teaspoon of the mixture into each mould. Bake for around 10 minutes until the florentines attain a lovely, golden brown. • While the florentines are baking, slowly melt the chocolate in a bowl placed over a pan of hot water (bain marie). • Allow the florentines to cool a little after baking before placing them on a mesh cooling rack. • Wash the baking tins, dry and place on the baking tray/mesh once more. • Put ½ teaspoon of melted chocolate into each tin/form. Gently knock the baking tray/mesh against the work counter so that the chocolate is evenly spread out. Now place the florentines on top of the soft chocolate and put into the fridge to cool for 2 hours.

Note • Do not bake the florentines for longer than 10 minutes, even if you think they are

Glasierte Nuss Steine

Backzeit: 20 Minuten • *Temperatur:* 180°

Zutaten • 3 Eiweiß • 140 g Zucker • 70 g Mehl • 140 g temperierte Butter
• 150 g gemahlene Walnüsse

Glasur • 120 g Puderzucker • 3 Eigelb • 1/2 Päckchen Vanillezucker

Zubereitung

• Zucker und temperierte Butter mischen. • Eiweiß steif schlagen und vorsichtig unter die Zucker-Buttermasse heben. • Danach gemahlene Nüsse und Mehl nach und nach ebenfalls vorsichtig unter den Teig heben. • Backofen auf 180° vorheizen. • Teig 2 cm dick in eine rechteckige Backform geben und mit einer Spatel gleichmäßig verteilen. • 20 Minuten bei 180° backen. • Glasur • Eigelb, Puderzucker und Vanillezucker lange zu Schaum schlagen. • Nach dem Backen sofort damit bestreichen. • Danach 25 Minuten ruhen lassen und danach die Glasur in Schnittengröße markieren. • Den Kuchen 2 Stunden ruhen lassen und aus der Form nehmen. • Kuchen auf ein Brett legen und Schnitten an den vormarkierten Stellen ausschneiden.

Glazed Nutty Rocks

Baking time: 20 minutes • *Temperature:* 180°C

Ingredients • 3 egg whites • 140 g sugar • 70 g flour • 140 g softened butter
• 150 g ground walnuts

Glaze • 120 g icing sugar • 3 egg yolks • 1/2 packet vanilla sugar

Preparation

• Mix together the sugar and softened butter. • Beat the egg white until stiff and carefully fold it into the sugar and butter mixture. • Slowly add in the ground nuts and flour, bit by bit. • Preheat the oven to 180°C. • Pour the mixture into a 2 cm deep rectangular baking tin and spread out evenly with a spatula. • Bake for 20 minutes at 180°C. • Glaze • Whisk the egg yolks, icing sugar and vanilla sugar until creamy. Brush over the pastry as soon as it has finished baking. • Leave to rest for 25 minutes and then mark out the slices in the glaze. • Leave the cake to rest for 2 hours and then remove from the tin. • Place the cake on a tray and cut along the pre-marked lines.

Gefüllte Tricorne

Ruhezeit: 1 Stunde • *Backzeit:* 15-20 Minuten • *Temperatur:* 180°

Zutaten • 500 g Mehl • 250 g Zucker • 250 g temperierte Butter • 3 Eigelb
• 1 Suppenlöffel Crème Fraiche

Füllung • 3 Eiweiß • 125 g Zucker • 125 g gemahlene Mandeln oder Haselnüsse
• *Variante:* Man kann die Füllung auch mit Marmelade ersetzen.

Glasur • 1 Ei (Eiweiß und Eigelb trennen)

Zubereitung

• Temperierte Butter und Zucker zu einer schaumigen Masse schlagen. • Nach und nach Eigelb und Crème Fraiche dazu geben. • Danach gesiebtes Mehl nach und nach darunter heben und zu einer homogenen Masse verarbeiten. • Teig in Kugelform in Frischhaltefolie 1 Stunde im Kühlen ruhen lassen. • Teig aus dem Kühlen nehmen und die Füllung vorbereiten. • Eiweiß zu Schnee schlagen. Nach und nach Zucker dazu geben und weiter zu einer festen Masse schlagen. • Die gemahlenen Mandeln / Haselnüsse vorsichtig mit einer Spatel unter das Eiweiß heben • Teig ausrollen und mit einer Form (ca. 6 cm Durchmesser) ausstechen. • Mittig auf die Plätzchen ein Häufchen der Füllung geben. • Den äußeren Rand der Plätzchen mit Eiweiß bestreichen und die Ränder zu einer Tricorne hochklappen. • Danach Tricorne mit Eigelb bestreichen und im Kühlen 30 Minuten ruhen lassen. • Backofen auf 180° vorheizen. • Tricorne ca 15-20 Minuten backen.

Stuffed Tricorns

Resting time: 1 hour • **Baking time:** 15-20 minutes • **Temperature:** 180°C

Ingredients • 500 g flour • 250 g sugar • 250 g softened butter • 3 egg yolks
• 1 tablespoon creme fraiche

Filling • 3 egg whites • 125 g sugar • 125 g ground almonds or hazelnuts
• **Variation:** Jam/marmalade can also be used for the filling.

• 1 egg (separate out the egg white and the yolk)

Preparation

• Whisk the softened butter and sugar until creamy. • Slowly add in the egg yolks and crème fraiche bit by bit. • Then fold in the sifted flour and work into a smooth dough. • Shape the dough into a ball, cover in cling film and leave to rest for 1 hour in a cool place. • Retrieve the dough from its resting place and prepare the filling. • Whisk the egg whites until fluffy. Add in the sugar bit by bit and beat until stiff. • Carefully fold the ground almonds/hazelnuts into the egg whites with a spatula. • Roll out the dough and cut into circles using a c. 6-cm diameter pastry cutter. • Place a mound of filling in the centre of each circle. • Brush the outer edges of the circles with egg white and fold over to form a tricorn shape. • Brush more egg white over the tricorns and leave to rest for 30 minutes in a cool place. • Preheat the oven to 180°C. • Bake the tricorns for about 15-20 minutes.

Haselnusshalbmonde

Backzeit: 15 Minuten • **Temperatur:** 175°

Zutaten • 250 g Mehl • 175 g temperierte Butter • 120 g gemahlene Haselnüsse • 1 Päckchen Vanillezucker • 100 g Zucker

Dekoration • Schokoladencouverture

Zubereitung

• Alle Zutaten zu einer homogenen Masse kneten. • Teig zu einer 4 cm dicken Wurst rollen. Davon 5 mm dicke Scheiben schneiden und zu kleinen Halbmonden formen. • Backofen auf 175° vorheizen. 15 Minuten backen. • Nach dem Erkalten eine Hälfte des Halbmondes in die zergangene Couverture tunken.

Hazelnut Crescents

Baking time: 15 minutes • **Temperature:** 175°C

Ingredients • 250 g flour • 175 g softened butter • 120 g ground hazelnuts • 1 packet vanilla sugar • 100 g sugar

Decoration • Chocolate coating

Preparation

• Knead all the ingredients together into a smooth dough. • Roll out the dough into a 4 cm thick sausage. Cut this into 5 mm thick slices and shape these into small crescents. • Preheat the oven to 175°C. Bake for 15 minutes. 15 Minuten backen. • After cooling, dip the crescents halfway into the melted chocolate.

Hefebrezel

Ruhezeit: *2 x 20 Minuten und 1 x 40 Minuten* • **Backzeit:** *30 Minuten*
• **Temperatur:** *190°*

Zutaten • *550 g Mehl* • *1 Päckchen Trockenhefe* • *3 Eier* • *100 g Zucker* • *150 g Butter*
• *150 g lauwarme Milch* • *10 g Salz* • **Bestreichen** • *1 ganzes Ei verrührt mit einer Prise Salz*

Zubereitung

• In der Teigmaschine Mehl und Trockenhefe mischen. • Danach Eier, warme Milch (37°),
Salz und Zucker dazugeben. • Alles gut mischen und zuletzt Butter in kleinen Stückchen
geschnitten hinzufügen. • Die Masse 5 Minuten kneten. • Den Teig abdecken und in einer
Schüssel 20 Minuten gehen lassen. • Danach den Teig nochmals schlagen und ein zweites Mal
20 Minuten gehen lassen. • Den Teig jetzt nochmals schlagen und zu einer 1,5 Meter langen
Wurst rollen. • Die Wurst zu einer Schleife legen und die Extremitäten (Enden) mittig
zu einer Brezel formen. • Die Endstücke mit lauwarmem Wasser ankleben. • Brezel auf
Backpapier oder Silikonfolie legen. • Noch einmal 40 Minuten gehen lassen. • Backofen auf
190° vorheizen. • Brezel mit geschlagenem Ei bestreichen. • Ungefähr 30 Minuten backen.
• Ratschlag: Manche Trockenhefe beinhaltet bereits Salz. Salz bräuchte somit nicht mehr
hinzugefügt werden.

Barm Pretzels

Resting time: 2 x 20 minutes and 1 x 40 minutes • **Baking time:** 30 minutes
• **Temperature:** 190°C

Ingredients • 550 g flour • 1 packet dried yeast • 3 eggs • 100 g sugar • 150 g butter
• 150 g lukewarm milk • 10 g salt

Glaze • 1 whole egg mixed with a pinch of salt

Preparation

• Combine the flour and dried yeast in a mixing machine. Add in the eggs, warm milk (37°C), salt and sugar. Mix everything together well and then slowly introduce the butter broken into small pieces. • Knead the mixture for 5 minutes, cover the dough and leave to rise in a bowl for 20 minutes. Knead the dough once more and leave to rise for a further 20 minutes. • Knead the dough a couple of times more and then roll into a 1.5 m long sausage. Tie the sausage into a loop and bring the ends in to the middle to form a pretzel shape. Wet the ends with lukewarm water and stick down. • Place the pretzel onto baking paper or a silicone sheet. Leave to rise for 40 minutes. • Preheat the oven to 190°C. • Glaze the pretzel with the beaten egg. • Bake for about 30 minutes. • Note: Some dried yeast already contains salt. If this is the case, no extra salt is needed.

Husarenknöpfe

Ruhezeit: 1 Stunde • *Backzeit:* 15 Minuten • *Temperatur:* 150°

Zutaten • 200 g temperierte Butter • 100 g Zucker • 1 Päckchen Vanillezucker • 2 Eigelb • 80 g gemahlene Haselnüsse • 300 g gesiebtes Mehl

Dekoration • 100 g Johannisbeergelee

Zubereitung

• Temperierte Butter, Zucker und Vanillezucker schaumig schlagen. • Eigelb, gemahlene Haselnüsse und zuletzt das gesiebte Mehl darunter heben. • Teig zu einer Kugel formen und in einer Frischhaltefolie 1 Stunde kalt stellen. • Backofen auf 150° vorheizen. • Nussgroße Kugeln formen und mit dem Finger eine Mulde mittig eindrücken und mit Johannisbeergelee füllen. • Auch andere Marmeladen sind möglich. • Husarenknöpfe auf Backpapier oder Silikonfolie legen und 15 Minuten bei 150° backen. • Nach dem Backen auf ein Gitter setzen und nach dem Abkühlen mit Puderzucker bestäuben. • **Variante** • Anstelle von Gelee oder Marmelade kann man glacierte Kirschen nehmen und nach dem Backen in die Mulde setzen.

Hussar Buttons

Resting time: 1 hour • *Baking time:* 15 minutes • *Temperature:* 150°C

Ingredients • 200 g softened butter • 100 g sugar • 1 packet vanilla sugar • 2 egg yolks • 80 g ground hazelnuts • 300 g sifted flour

Decoration • 100 g redcurrant jelly

Preparation

• Whisk together the softened butter, sugar and vanilla sugar until creamy. • Fold in the egg yolks, ground hazelnuts and, finally, the sifted flour. • Form the dough into a ball, cover in cling film and leave to rest for 1 hour in a cool place. • Preheat the oven to 150°C. • Shape the dough into nut-sized balls. Form a dip in the centre of each with your finger and fill with redcurrant jelly (or a different jam, if preferred). • Place the "Hussar Buttons" on baking paper or silicone sheet and bake for 15 minutes at 150°C. • After baking, place on a mesh rack to cool. Once cool, dust with icing sugar.

Variante • Instead of jelly or jam, put glacé cherries in the dips after baking.

Lebkuchenzüngle

Ruhezeit: *Minimum eine Nacht* • **Backzeit:** *10-12 Minuten* • **Temperatur:** *180°*

Zutaten • *250 g Zucker* • *50 g Butter* • *165 g Tannenhonig* • *2 große Eier* • *1 Kaffeelöffel Zimt* • *1 Teelöffel gemahlene Nelken* • *1 Kaffeelöffel Bikarbonat (Natron)* • *580 g Mehl* • *1/2 Päckchen Backpulver* • *60 g gehakte Walnüsse* • *1 Schuss Kirschwasser*

Alternativ: *In kleine Würfel geschnittene Orangeade und Zitronade*

Glasur • *2 Eiweiß* • *300 g Puderzucker*

Zubereitung

Am Vorabend • Honig, Zucker und Butter in einem großen Kochtopf zergehen und danach abkühlen lassen. • Eier, Zimt gemahlene Nelken und Natron (zuerst in kaltem Wasser aufgehen lassen) darunter mischen. • Danach Mehl, Backpulver, gemahlene Walnüsse und Kirschwasser dazugeben. • Den Teig zu einer Kugel formen und in einer Frischhaltefolie im Kühlen ruhen lassen. • Mindestens eine Nacht oder sogar etwas länger.

Am nächsten Tag • Den Teig mindestens 1 Stunde vor der Weiterbearbeitung bei Zimmertemperatur stehen lassen. • Backofen auf 180° vorheizen. • Teig auf bemehlte Fläche 2 cm dich ausrollen und mit einem Lebkuchenausstecher Züngle ausstechen. • 10-12 Minuten backen. • Die Lebkuchenzüngle müssen danach immer noch etwas weich sein (sie werden fest bei Zimmertemperatur). • Danach Züngle mit der Glasur bestreichen und trocknen lassen.

Spiced Cat's Tongues

Resting time: minimum 1 night • *Baking time:* 10-12 minutes • *Temperature:* 180°C

Ingredients • 250 g sugar • 50 g butter • 165 g pine honey • 2 large eggs • 1/2 teaspoon cinnamon • 1 teaspoon ground cloves • 1/2 teaspoon bicarbonate of soda (Natron) • 580 g flour • 1/2 packet baking powder • 60 g chopped walnuts • A dash of cherry brandy

Alternativ: Finely chopped orange and lemon peel

Icing • 2 egg whites • 300 g icing sugar

Preparation

One day in advance • Melt the honey, sugar and butter together in a large saucepan and then leave to cool. • Stir in the eggs, cinnamon, ground cloves and bicarbonate of soda (dissolve in cold water beforehand), then add in the flour, baking powder, ground walnuts and cherry brandy. • Shape the dough into a ball, wrap it in cling film and leave to rest in a cool place for a night at least or longer.

The next day • Before doing anything further, leave the dough to stand at room temperature for at least 1 hour. • Preheat the oven to 180°C. • Roll out the dough on a flour-covered surface until it is 2cm thick then cut out the biscuits using a cutter. • Bake for 10-12 minutes. • After baking, the Lebkuchen biscuits will feel a little soft (they will harden once cooled to room temperature). • Once the biscuits are cool, cover with icing and leave to dry.

Leckerli

Backzeit: 18 Minuten • **Temperatur:** 190°

Zutaten • 375 g Mehl • 125 g Zucker • 200 g gut flüssiger Honig • 1/2 Kaffeelöffel Lebkuchengewürz • 1 Päckchen Backpulver • 300 ml Schnaps • 100 g gehakte Mandeln • 50 g kandierte Orangenschale • 50 g Zitronenschale • 5 cl Milch

Glasur • 200 g Puderzucker • 20 ml Schnaps

Zubereitung

• Backofen auf 180° vorheizen. • Mehl, Zucker, Backpulver, gehakte Mandeln, kandierte Früchte und Lebkuchengewürz gut mischen. • Honig und Schnaps dazugeben und zu einem Teig verarbeiten. • Danach die Milch hinzufügen, um den Teig weiterhin gut verarbeiten zu können. • Masse in gefettete Back- oder Silikonform mit einem Rand von ca 2 cm Höhe geben. • Mit einem gemehlten Walholz leicht über den Teig gleiten, damit er gleichmäßig hoch ist. • 18 Minuten backen. • Der Teig darf nicht zu braun werden, sonst wird er gegebenenfalls zu fest. • Nach dem Backen den Teig auf ein Holzbrett legen und mit der Glasur bestreichen. • Trocknen lassen. • Nach dem Erkalten quadratische oder rechteckige Stücke schneiden.

Yummies

Baking time: 18 minutes • **Temperature:** 190°C

Ingredients • 375 g flour • 125 g sugar • 200 g good quality, runny honey • 1/4 teaspoon Lebkuchen spice • 1 packet baking powder • 300 ml Schnapps • 100 g chopped almonds • 50 g candied orange peel • 50 g lemon peel • 5 cl milk

Icing • 200 g icing sugar • 20 ml Schnapps

Preparation

• Preheat the oven to 180°C. • Mix the flour, sugar, baking powder, chopped almonds, candied fruit and Lebkuchen spice together well. • Add in the honey and Schnapps, then knead into a dough. Pour in the milk as required to keep working the dough. • Put the mixture into a 2 cm deep greased baking tin or silicone form. Use a rolling pin lightly dusted with flour, to flatten out the dough. • Bake for 18 minutes. • Don't let the dough get too brown, or it will be too hard. After baking, transfer the pastry onto a board and cover with the icing. Leave to dry. When cool, cut into squares or rectangles.

Liebestaler

Backzeit: *8-10 Minuten* • **Temperatur:** *210°*

Zutaten • *125 g temperierte Butter* • *125 g Zucker* • *1 Päckchen Vanillezucker* • *150 g Mehl* • *80 g in Rum eingelegte Corinthen* • *2 Eier* • *1 Prise Salz*

Zubereitung

• Corinthen am Abend zuvor in Rum einlegen. • Temperierte Butter, Zucker und Salz gut verrühren. • Die Eier nach und nach dazu geben. • Danach Mehl unter die Masse rühren und zuletzt die Corinthen dazu geben. • Backofen auf 210° vorheizen. • Mit 2 Kaffeelöffeln kleine Häufchen auf das Backpapier oder Silikonfolie geben. Dabei genügend Abstand dazwischen lassen, da sich die Masse bei der Wärme ausbreitet. • Backen bis der Rand der Taler schön braun ist. • Das Innere der Taler muss noch etwas weich sein.

Love Coins

Baking time: *8-10 minutes* • **Temperature:** *210°C*

Ingredients • *125 g softened butter* • *125 g sugar* • *1 packet vanilla sugar* • *150 g flour* • *80 g rum-soaked currants* • *2 eggs* • *1 pinch salt*

Preparation

• Cover the currants with rum and leave to soak overnight. • The following day: Thoroughly mix together the softened butter, sugar and salt. • Slowly add in the eggs, bit by bit. • Now fold in the flour and, finally, stir in the currants. • Preheat the oven to 210°C. • Using two teaspoons, make little mounds on baking paper or silicone sheet, leaving enough space for the dough to spread during cooking. • Bake until the biscuit edges are a beautiful golden brown. • The centre of the coins should still be slightly soft.

Makronen-Sandplätzchen mit Himbeermarmelade

Backzeit: *15 Minuten* • **Temperatur:** *175°*

Zutaten • **Sandgebäckteig** • *125 g Mehl* • *125 g Zucker* • *125 g temperierte Butter* • *120 g gemahlene Haselnüsse* • *125 g Paniermehl* • *1 Ei* • *Eine geraspelte Zitronenschale* • *Eine Messerspitze gemahlene Nelken* • *Eine Messerspitze Zimt* • *Eine Messerspitze Muskatnuss*

Haselnussmakronenteig • *120 g gemahlene Haselnuss* • *20 g Mehl* • *180 g Eiweiß* • *150 g Zucker* • *1/2 Kaffeelöffel Zimt* • *1 Glas Himbeermarmelade* • *Puderzucker*

Zubereitung

Sandgebäckteig • Alle Zutaten, außer dem Ei, zwischen den Händen zu einem Teig reiben. • Ei dazugeben und zu einem Teig kneten. • Teig 2-3 Stunden in Frischhaltefolie ins Kühle stellen. • Teig 4 mm dick ausrollen. • Mit einer Form Plätzchen ausstechen. Himbeermarmelade mittig auf die Plätzchen geben.

Haselnussmakronenteig • Eiweiß und Zucker zu festem Schnee schlagen. • Vorsichtig mit einer Spatel Mehl, gemahlene Haselnüsse und Zimt darunter heben. • Die Masse in einen Spritzbeutel geben und häufchenweise auf die Marmeladen-Plätzchen spritzen. • Mit Puderzucker bestäuben. • Backofen auf 175° vorheizen. 15 Minuten backen.

Macaroon Sponge Cakes with Raspberry Jam

Baking time: 15 minutes • Temperature: 175°C

*Ingredients • **For the sponge** • 125 g flour • 125 g sugar • 125 g softened butter • 120 g ground hazelnuts • 125 g breadcrumbs • 1 egg • Grated rind of 1 lemon • 1 pinch ground cloves • 1 pinch cinnamon • 1 pinch nutmeg*

***For the hazelnut macaroon** • 120 g ground hazelnut • 20 g flour • 180 g egg white • 150 g sugar • 1/4 teaspoon cinnamon • 1 jar raspberry jam • Icing sugar*

Preparation

Sponge mixture • Using your hands, evenly mix together all the ingredients, apart from the egg. • Add in the egg and knead into a dough. • Cover the dough with cling film and leave to rest for 2-3 hours in a cool place. • Roll out the dough until it is 4 mm thick. • Cut out the biscuits, using a pastry cutter. Place some raspberry jam in the centre of each biscuit.

Hazelnut Macaroon mixture • Whisk the egg white and sugar until firm and fluffy. • Gently fold in the flour, ground hazelnuts and cinnamon with a spatula. • Spoon the mixture into a piping bag and squeeze a small mound onto each jam biscuit. • Dust with icing sugar. • Preheat the oven to 175°C. Bake for 15 minutes.

Männele

Ruhezeit: 1 x 30 Minuten und 1 x 40 Minuten • **Backzeit:** 15-18 Minuten
• **Temperatur:** 190°

Zutaten • 500 g Mehl • 1 Päckchen Trockenhefe • 100 g Zucker • 100 g Butter • 2 ganze Eier • 100 g Corinthen • 200 g lauwarme Milch (37°) • 10 g Salz

Bestreichen zum Bräunen • 1 Ei • 1 Prise Salz

Zubereitung

• In einer Teigmaschine Mehl und Trockenhefe mischen. • Danach Zucker, Eier, lauwarme Milch und Salz dazugeben. • Alles 1 Minute mit der Maschine schlagen und danach Butterflocken dazugeben und nochmals 4 Minuten schlagen. • Den Teig 30 Minuten gehen lassen und danach mit der Hand schlagen.

Männle formen • Teig in 4 Stücke teilen. Danach jedes Viertel in 3 Teile teilen. • Die Teigstückle längs auswalen. • Mit einer Schere die Teiglinge von unten bis zur Hälfte auseinander schneiden, um die Beine zu formen. • Beide Seiten einschneiden, um die Arme zu formen. • Danach im oberen Teil wieder einschneiden, um den Kopf zu formen. • Männele auf Backpapier oder Silikonfolie legen. • 2 Corinthen in den Kopf setzen für die Augen, 2 oder 3 Corinthen im Bauchbereich als Knöpfe. • Die Männele nochmals 40 Minuten gehen lassen. • Backofen auf 190° vorheizen. • Männele zum Bräunen mit Ei bestreichen. Backzeit 15-18 Minuten.

Beachten • Manche Trockenhefe beinhaltet bereits Salz. • Salz braucht dann nicht mehr hinzugefügt werden.

Little Men

Resting time: 1 x 30 minutes and 1 x 40 minutes • *Baking time:* 15-18 minutes
• *Temperature:* 190°C

Ingredients • 500 g flour • 1 sachet dried yeast • 100 g sugar • 100 g butter • 2 whole eggs
• 100 g currants • 200 g lukewarm milk (37°C) • 10 g salt

Glaze for browning • 1 egg • 1 pinch salt

Preparation

• Combine the flour and dried yeast in a mixing machine. • Then add in the sugar, eggs, lukewarm milk and salt. • Mix everything together in the machine for about 1 minute and then introduce flakes of butter and whisk for a further 4 minutes. • Leave the dough to rise for 30 minutes and then knead by hand.

Forming the « Little Men »: Cut the dough into 4 pieces. • Separate each quarter into 3 pieces. • Roll out the pieces of dough lengthways. • Using scissors, cut each piece from the bottom halfway up to form the legs. • Next, cut into the dough on both sides to form the arms and finally, cut out a head at the top. • Lay the figures on baking paper or a silicone sheet. • Place two currants for eyes and 2 or 3 currants on the body for buttons. • Leave to rise for a further 40 minutes. • Preheat the oven to 190°C. • Brush egg onto the biscuits to brown them.

Note • Some dried yeast already contains salt. If this is the case, no extra salt is needed.

Mini Linzer

Ruhezeit: *2 Stunden ruhen lassen* • **Backen:** *15-18 Minuten* • **Temperatur:** *175°*

Zutaten • *250 g Mehl* • *250 g temperierte Butter* • *125 g Zucker* • *1 Ei* • *1 Eigelb*
• *250 g gemahlene Mandeln oder Haselnüsse* • *15 g Zimt* • *1 Prise Salz*

Garnitur • *Glas Himbeermarmelade*

Zubereitung • Mehl, Salz Butter, Zimt, Mandeln/Haselnüsse zusammen mischen.
• Danach die Butter dazu geben. • Den Teig mit den Fingern zusammen kneten
• Ei und Eigelb dazu geben und zu einer homogenen Masse weiter verarbeiten. • Zu
einer Kugel formen und in einer Frischhaltefolie 2 Stunden im Kühlen ruhen lassen.
• Backofen auf 175° vorheizen. • Teig ausrollen und mit einer runden oder gezackten
Form ausstechen. • Die Hälfte der Plätzchen mit einem Fingerhut oder Apfelausstecher
mittig ausstechen. • Die ganzen Plätzchen auf ein Backpapier oder Silikonfolie legen.
• Danach eine nussgroße Marmeladenmenge in die Mitte des Plätzchens aufbringen und
das ausgestochene Plätzchen darauf geben. • Die Mini-Linzer 15-18 Minuten bei 175°
backen. • Nach dem Backen auf einem Gitter auskühlen lassen.

Variante • Man kann auch kleine Teigkugeln formen, mit dem Zeigefinger eine Kuhle
hineindrücken und mit Marmelade füllen.

Mini Linzer Biscuits

Resting time: 2 hours • *Baking time:* 15-18 minutes • *Temperature:* 175°C

Ingredients • 250 g flour • 250 g softened butter • 125 g sugar • 1 egg • 1 egg yolk • 250 g ground almonds or hazelnuts • 15 g cinnamon • 1 pinch salt

Coating • Jar of raspberry jam

Preparation

• Mix together the flour, salt, butter, cinnamon and almonds/hazelnuts. • Add in the butter. • Knead with your fingers. • Add in the egg and egg yolk and work into a smooth dough. • Form the dough into a ball, cover in cling film and leave to rest for 2 hours in a cool place. • Preheat the oven to 175°C. • Roll out the dough and cut using a serrated pastry cutter. • Cut out shapes in the centre of half the pieces with a thimble or apple corer to form the lids. • Place the remaining pieces on baking paper or silicone sheet. • Place a blob of jam in the centre of each of these (about the size of a nut) and place the cut lids over them. • Bake the Mini-Linzer for 15-18 minutes at 175°C. • After baking, leave to cool on a cooling tray/mesh.

Variation • Another method is to make small doughballs, create a well in each ball with a finger and fill these with jam.

Schokoladenmakronen

Backzeit: *15 Minuten* • **Temperatur:** *160°*

Zutaten • *125 g schwarze Schokolade* • *125 g gemahlene Haselnüsse oder Mandeln* • *125 g Puderzucker* • *1 Ei* • *1 Päckchen Vanillezucker*

Zubereitung

• Schokolade im Wasserbad zergehen lassen. • Eier, Puderzucker und Vanillezucker schaumig rühren. • Geschmolzene Schokolade, Mandeln / Haselnüsse dazu geben. • Backofen auf 160° vorheizen. • Die Masse in einen Spritzbeutel mit gezacktem Einsatz (ca. 14 mm Durchmesser) füllen oder mit 2 Kaffeelöffeln kleine Häufchen auf das Backpapier oder Silikonfolie spritzen. • 15 Minuten bei 160° backen.

Empfehlung • Die Makronen müssen innen noch etwas weich sein. • Auf dem Backpapier gut erkalten lassen bevor man sie herunter nimmt. • Falls man die doppelte Menge an Makronen machen will, muss man die noch nicht verarbeitete Teigmasse über dem Wasserbad weich halten.

Chocolate Macaroons

Baking time: 15 minutes • **Temperature:** 160°C

Ingredients • 125 g dark chocolate • 125 g ground hazelnuts or almonds • 125 g icing sugar • 1 egg • 1 packet vanilla sugar

Preparation

• Melt the chocolate in a bowl over a pan of hot water (bain marie). • Mix together the eggs, icing sugar and vanilla sugar until creamy. • Add in the melted chocolate and almonds/hazelnuts. • Preheat the oven to 160°C. • Spoon the mixture into a piping bag with a serrated nozzle (about 14 mm diameter), or use two teaspoons to create small mounds on baking paper or silicone sheet. • Bake for 15 minutes at 160°C.

Note • The macaroons will be rather soft still. Leave them to cool down properly before removing them from the baking paper.• If you are making double the amount of macaroons, keep the remaining dough soft by putting it in the bain marie.

Schokoladenrosette

Backzeit: *10-15 Minuten* • **Temperatur:** *180° - 190°*

Zutaten • *300 g temperierte Butter* • *250 g Puderzucker* • *4 Eier* • *500 g gesiebtes Mehl* • *25 g Kakao* • *1 Prise Salz* • *1/2 Kaffeelöffel Backpulver*

Dekoration • *Schokoladenkugeln*

Zubereitung

• Mehl, Backpulver, Kakao sieben. • Butter, Zuker und Salz verrühren. • Nach und nach die Eier dazugeben. • Mehlmischung vorsichtig unter die Masse heben. • Teig in den Spritzbeutel geben. Rosetten auf Backpapier oder Silikonfolie spitzen. Mittig in jede Rosette ein Schokoladenkügelchen setzen. • Backofen auf 180°-190° vorheizen. • 10-15 Minuten Backen.

Chocolate Rosettes

Baking time: *10-15 minutes* • **Temperature:** *180°-190°C*

Ingredients • *300 g softened butter* • *250 g icing sugar* • *4 eggs* • *500 g sifted flour* • *25 g cocoa* • *1 pinch salt* • *1/4 teaspoon baking powder*

Decoration • *Chocolate balls*

Preparation

• Sift together the flour, baking powder and cocoa in a bowl. • In a separate bowl, mix together the butter, sugar and salt. • Slowly add in the eggs bit by bit. • Carefully fold in the flour mixture. • Using a piping bag, make rosette shapes on baking paper or silicone sheet. Place a chocolate ball in the centre of each rosette. • Preheat the oven to 180°-190°C. • Bake for 10-15 Minutes.

Schokoladenzüngle

Backen: *10-15 Minuten* • **Temperatur:** *180°*

Zutaten • *125 g Butter* • *100 g Zucker* • *1 Ei* • *1 Päckchen Vanillezucker* • *150 g Mehl* • *100 g gemahlene Haselnüsse*

Garnitur • *150 g schwarze Schokolade*

Zubereitung

• Den Backofen auf 180° vorheizen. • Butter und Zucker schaumig schlagen. • Ei, Vanillezucker, gemahlene Haselnüsse und Mehl darunter heben. • Teig in den Spritzbeutel geben und in Züngleform auf Backpapier oder Silikonfolie spritzen. • 10-15 Minuten backen. • Züngle erkalten lassen.

Garnitur • Schokolade im Wasserbad zergehen lassen und die Züngle hälftig in die Schokolade tunken. • Danach auf einem Gitter trocknen lassen.

Chocolate Cat Tongues

Baking time: *10-15 minutes* • **Temperature:** *180°C*

Ingredients • *125 g butter* • *100 g sugar* • *1 egg* • *1 packet vanilla sugar* • *150 g flour* • *100 g ground hazelnuts*

Coating • *150 g dark chocolate*

Preparation

• Preheat the oven to 180°C. • Whisk together the butter and sugar until creamy. • Fold in the egg, vanilla sugar, ground hazelnuts and flour. • Spoon the mixture into a piping bag and pipe tongue shapes onto baking paper or silicone sheet. • Bake for 10-15 minutes. • Leave the biscuits to cool.

Coating • Melt the chocolate in a bowl over a pan of hot water (bain marie). Dip the biscuits halfway into the chocolate. • Leave to harden on a cooling tray/mesh.

Schwowebredele

Ruhezeit: | Nacht • *Backzeit:* 10-15 Minuten • *Temperatur:* 180°

Zutaten • *500 g Mehl* • *270 g temperierte Butter* • *2 Eier* • *250 g Zucker* • *150 g gemahlene Mandeln oder Haselnüsse* • *| Prise Salz* • *20 g Zimt* • *Abgeriebene Zitronenschale*

Garnitur • | Ei

Zubereitung

• Temperierte Butter und Mehl zusammen kneten. • Eier, Zucker, Zimt, Gemahlene Mandeln/ Haselnüsse, abgeriebene Zitronenschale dazu geben und zu einer homogenen Masse verarbeiten. • Teig in eine Frischhaltefolie wickeln und eine Nacht im Kühlen ruhen lassen. • Am nächsten Tag eine halbe Stunde vor der Weiterbearbeitung in Zimmertemperatur stehen lassen • Teig ausrollen in 3-4 mm • Backofen auf 180° vorheizen. • Mit verschiedenen Formen Plätzchen ausstechen. • Die Plätzchen auf ein Backpapier oder Silikonfolie legen. • Plätzchen mit dem gut zerschlagenen Ei bestreichen, trocknen lassen und danach ein zweites Mal bestreichen. • 10-15 Minuten backen auf 180° backen.

Schwobebredele

Resting time: | night • *Baking time:* 10-15 minutes • *Temperature:* 180°C

Ingredients • *500 g flour* • *270 g softened butter* • *2 eggs* • *250 g sugar* • *150 g ground almonds or hazelnuts* • *| pinch salt* • *20 g cinnamon* • *Grated lemon rind*

Glaze • | Egg

Preparation

• Knead together the softened butter and flour. • Fold in the eggs, sugar, cinnamon, ground almonds/hazelnuts, grated lemon rind and work into a smooth dough. • Wrap the dough in cling film and leave to rest overnight in a cool place. • The following day, before continuing, leave to stand for half an hour at room temperature. • Roll out the dough to a depth of 3-4 mm. • Preheat the oven to 180°C. • Cut out the biscuits using a variety of shapes. • Lay them out on baking paper or silicone sheet. • Brush the well-whisked egg whites over the biscuits, leave to dry and then brush over once more. • Bake for 10-15 minutes at 180°C.

Schweizer Sandgebäck

Backzeit: *10-12 Minuten* • **Temperatur:** *180°*

Zutaten • **Sandteig natur** • *600 g gesiebtes Mehl* • *400 g temperierte Butter*
• *300 g Puderzucker* • *1 Ei*

Schokoladensandteig • *600 g gesiebtes Mehl* • *60 g Kakao* • *400 g temperierte Butter*
• *300 g Puderzucker* • *2 Eier*

Zum Bestreichen • *1 Ei*

Zubereitung

Sandteig natur • Mehl sieben. • Alle Zutaten, außer dem Ei, zwischen den Händen reiben. Ei dazugeben und zu einer homogenen Masse kneten. • Teig 3-4 Stunden in einer Frischehaltefolie im Kühlen ruhen lassen.

Schokoladensandteig • Dieselbe Verarbeitung wie beim Sandteig natur. • Sandteig 3 cm dick ausrollen. • Dasselbe für Schokoladensandteig. • Danach zwei gleichmäßige Rechtecke schneiden. • Natursandteig mit Eigelb bestreichen. • Schokoladensandteig darauf legen und ebenfalls mit Eigelb bestreichen. • Den Teig zu einer 3 cm dicken Wurst formen und in einer Frischhaltefolie 3-4 Stunden im Kühlen ruhen lassen. • 5 mm dicke Scheiben schneiden. • Sandplätzchen auf Backpapier oder Silikonfolie legen. • Backofen auf 180° vorheizen. • 10-12 Minuten backen.

Swiss Sponge Cakes

Baking time: *10-12 minutes* • **Temperature:** *180°C*

Ingredients • **For the plain sponge** • *600 g sifted flour* • *400 g softened butter* • *300 g icing sugar* • *1 egg*

For the chocolate sponge • *600 g sifted flour* • *60 g cocoa* • *400 g softened butter* • *300 g icing sugar* • *2 eggs*

Coating • *1 egg*

Preparation

Plain sponge • Sift the flour into a bowl. • Using your hands, mix together all the ingredients apart from the egg. Add in the egg and knead to form a smooth dough. • Cover the dough with cling film and leave to rest for 3-4 hours in a cool place.

Chocolate Sponge • Prepare in the same way as the plain sponge. • After resting. • Roll out the plain sponge dough until it is 3 cm thick. • The same applies to the chocolate sponge. • Cut out two equal sized rectangles. • Brush the plain sponge with the egg yolk. • Now lay the chocolate sponge over it and brush that with the egg yolk as well. • Roll the dough into a 3 cm thick sausage, cover in cling film and leave to rest for 3-4 hours in a cool place. • Cut into 5 mm thick slices. • Lay out the sponge cakes on baking paper or silicone sheet. • Preheat the oven to 180°C. Bake for 10-12 minutes.

Springerle

Backzeit: *12 Minuten* • **Temperatur:** *180°*

Zutaten • *Für ungefähr 500 gr Springerle* • *2 Eier oder 100 gr Eier* • *200 gr Zucker*
• *1 Päckchen Vanillezucker* • *270 gr Mehl* | *1 Messerspitze Backpulver* • *5 gr Aniskörner*

Zubereitung

• Eier, Zucker und Vanillezucker in einen Topf geben. • Topf auf den Herd stellen und die Mischung mit einem Schneebesen bis ca. 50° verrühren. • Die Mischung jetzt in eine Rührschüssel geben und mit dem Mixer ca. 10 Minuten schlagen bis sich die Masse verdoppelt hat. • Mehl und Backpulver sieben und mit den Aniskörnern unter die geschlagene Eier-Teigmasse heben. • Den Teig ca. 1 cm dick ausrollen und den Teig gut bemehlen, damit er nicht in den Formen kleben bleibt. • Die verschiedenen Springerformen fest auf den Teig drücken, damit die Bilder gut erkennbar sind. • Springerle danach sachte mit einem Pinsel vom Mehl entfernen. • Springerlebilder jetzt mit einem Messer oder einer runden oder viereckigen Form ausstechen. • Springerle auf ein Backblech mit Backpapier oder Silikonfolie legen und 2 Stunden an einem trockenen Ort krustig werden lassen (die Kruste muss genügend dick sein, damit sie krächelt, wenn man mit dem Finger darauf drückt). • Backofen auf 180° vorheizen, bei Ober- und Unterhitze 12 Minuten backen lassen bis sie eine leichte Farbe haben.

Zu wissen • Die Springerle haben oft ein Löchlein, damit man ein Band durchziehen kann zwecks Dekoration von einem Weihnachtsbaum oder Ähnlichem. Der Name Springerle kommt daher, weil sie aus der Form springen.

Little Jumpers or Little Knights

Baking time: 12 minutes • *Temperature:* 180°C

Ingredients • *For about 500 g of Springerle* • *2 eggs (or 100 g eggs)* • *200 g sugar* • *1 packet vanilla sugar* • *270 g flour* • *1 pinch baking powder* • *5 g aniseed*

Preparation

• Put the eggs, sugar and vanilla sugar in a saucepan. Place the pan on the stove and whisk the mixture by hand until it reaches a temperature of 50°C.

Now pour the mixture into a mixing bowl and whisk with an electric mixer until it doubles in size. • Sift together the flour and baking powder and fold into the egg/dough mixture together with the aniseed. • Roll out the dough until it is about 1 cm thick, and then dust it well with flour, so that it doesn't stick to the moulds. • Press different moulds firmly into the dough, so that the pictures are clearly recognisable. • Softly brush off the flour from the Springerle. • Cut out the individual Springerle pictures using a knife or round or square pastry cutter, as preferred. • Place the Springerle on a baking tray covered with baking paper or silicone sheet and leave for 2 hours in a dry place to form a crust (the crust must be thick enough to crackle when tapped). • Preheat the oven to 180°C and bake for 12 minutes until they are a delicate brown.

Note • The Springerle often have holes inserted so that they can be hung by a ribbon to decorate a Christmas tree or similar. They are called Springerle (Little Jumpers) because they spring or jump out of the moulds.

Spritzbredele

Ruhezeit: 1 Stunde • *Backzeit:* 15 Minuten • *Temperatur:* 180°

Zutaten • 500 g gesiebtes Mehl • 250 g temperierte Butter • 250 g Zucker • 5 Eigelb

Zubereitung

• Temperierte Butter, Zucker und Eigelbe gut schaumig rühren. • Gesiebtes Mehl dazu geben und zu einer guten homogenen Masse verarbeiten. • Teig zu einer Kugel formen und in einer Frischhaltefolie 1 Stunde im Kühlen ruhen lassen. • Danach den Teig nochmals bearbeiten. Teig in einen Fleischwolf mit einem speziellen Rauteneinsatz füllen und den Auswurf nach beliebiger Länge, auch in S-Form oder Kränzchen auf eine Backfolie legen. • Das Ganze geht auch mit einem Spritzbeutel. • Bei vorgeheiztem Backofen 15 Minuten bei 180° backen.

Christmas Biscuits

Resting time: 1 hour • *Baking time:* 15 minutes • *Temperature:* 180°C

Ingredients • 500 g sifted flour • 250 g softened butter • 250 g sugar • 5 egg yolks

Preparation

• Whisk together the softened butter, sugar and egg yolks until creamy. • Fold in the sifted flour and work up into a smooth dough. • Roll the dough into a ball, cover with cling film and leave to rest for 1 hour in a cool place. • After an hour, knead the dough once more. • Put the dough into a mincing machine with a special lozenge-shaped insert. As the dough emerges, cut it to your preferred length, and lay out on a baking sheet in rings or s-shapes. Alternatively, you can use a piping bag. • Bake in a preheated oven for 15 minutes at 180°C.

Süße Brezeln

Ruhen: *1 Stunde* • **Backen:** *12-15 Minuten* • **Temperatur:** *190°*

Zutaten • *500 g Mehl* • *180 g Zucker* • *2 Eier* • *200 g temperierte Butter*

Glasur • *150 g Puderzucker* • *1 Suppenlöffel Schnaps oder Zitronen- oder Orangensaft*

Utensilien (Zubehör): *Brezelausstecher*

Zubereitung

• Eier und Zucker zu einer schaumigen Masse schlagen. Butter dazu geben. Nach und nach das gesiebte Mehl. • Teig kneten und danach zu einer Kugel formen und in eine Frischhaltefolie wickeln. • Eine Stunde im Kühlen ruhen lassen. • Backofen auf 190° vorheizen. • Teig auswalzen und mit einer Brezelform ausstechen. Die Brezeln auf Backpapier oder Silikonfolie legen. • 12-15 Minuten backen. • Nach dem Backen die Glasur vorbereiten. • Zucker und Saft gut verrühren. • Brezeln mit der Glasur bestreichen und auf einem Backgitter trocknen lassen.

Sweet Pretzels

Resting time: *1 hour* • **Baking time:** *12-15 minutes* • **Temperature:** *190°C*

Ingredients • *500 g flour* • *180 g sugar* • *2 eggs* • *200 g softened butter*

Glaze • *150 g icing sugar* • *1 tablespoon Schnapps or lemon/orange juice*

Utensils (Equipment): *Pretzel cutter*

Preparation

• Whisk the eggs and sugar until creamy. • Add in the butter, and then slowly sift in the flour, bit by bit. • Knead the dough and shape into a ball, cover with cling film, then leave to rest for 1 hour in a cool place. • Preheat the oven to 190°C. • Roll out the dough and cut out the biscuits using a pretzel cutter. • Place the pretzels on baking paper or silicone sheet. • Bake for 12-15 minutes. • After baking, prepare the glaze. Thoroughly mix together the sugar and juice. • Brush the glaze mixture over the pretzels and leave to dry on a mesh cooling rack.

Vanille-Kipferle

Ruhezeit: 2 Stunden • **Backzeit:** *10-15 Minuten* • **Temperatur:** *190°*

Zutaten • *320 g Mehl* • *60 g gemahlene Haselnüsse* • *60 g gemahlene Mandeln* • *120 g Zucker* • *2 Eigelb* • *270 g temperierte Butter*

Bestreuen • *Feiner Zucker* • *2 Päckchen Vanillezucker*

Zubereitung

• Temperierte Butter und Zucker zu einer schaumigen Masse schlagen. • Eigelb nach und nach dazu geben. • Danach gemahlene Mandeln, Haselnüsse und Mehl darunter heben. • Teig zu einer Kugel formen und 2 Stunden im Kühlen in einer Frischhaltefolie ruhen lassen. • Backofen auf 190° vorheizen. • Aus dem Teig daumendicke Rollen formen, gut 2 cm lange Stücke davon abschneiden, diese zu etwa 5 cm langen Rollen formen. • Dabei die Enden etwas dünner rollen, als Hörnchen auf das Backpapier oder Silikonfolie auf ein Backblech legen. • 10-15 Minuten backen. • Die noch heißen Hörnchen in der Zuckermischung (feiner Zucker, Backpulver) wälzen.

Vanilla Crescents

Resting time: *2 hours* • **Baking time:** *10-15 minutes* • **Temperature:** *190°C*

Ingredients • *320 g flour* • *60 g ground hazelnuts* • *60 g ground almonds* • *120 g sugar* • *2 egg yolks* • *270 g softened butter*

For the coating • *Caster sugar* • *2 packets vanilla sugar*

Preparation

• Whisk together the softened butter and sugar until creamy. • Slowly introduce the egg yolks bit by bit. • Now fold in the almonds, hazelnuts and flour. • Form the dough into a ball, cover in cling film and leave to rest for 2 hours in a cool place. • Preheat the oven to 190°C. • Shape the dough into rolls about the width of a thumb, and cut these into 2 cm long pieces. Roll the pieces into 5 cm long rolls, narrowing at each end, and place them on baking paper or silicone sheet, curving them into crescents. • Bake for 10-15 minutes. Toss the hot crescents in the sugar mixture (caster sugar, vanilla sugar).

Weihnachtssterne mit Mandelbaiser (Meringe)

Ruhe: *1 Stunde* • **Backen:** *15-18 Minuten* • **Temperatur:** *170°*

Zutaten • *Sternenteig • 500 g Mehl • 250 g temperierte Butter • 6 Eigelb • 125 g Zucker*

Baisermasse (Meringe) • *3 Eiweiß • 125 g Zucker • 125 g gemahlene Mandeln*

Zubereitung

• Butter und Zucker schaumig rühren. • Eigelb darunter geben. Gesiebtes Mehl darunter heben. Zu einem glatten, homogenen Teig kneten. • Teig zu einer Kugel formen und in eine Frischhaltefolie wickeln und 1 Stunde im Kühlen ruhen lassen. • Teig 4 mm dick auswalzen. • Mit einer Sternenform ausstechen. Diese auf Backpapier oder Silikonfolie legen und ruhen lassen. • Backofen auf 150° vorheizen.

Baiser (Meringemasse) • Eiweiß zu Schnee schlagen. Bei mittlerer Festigkeit Zucker dazu geben und weiter zu einer festen Masse schlagen. • Gemahlene Mandeln mit einer Spachtel vorsichtig darunter heben. • Eischnee in eine Spritztüte füllen und mittig eine nussgroße Masse auf die Sternchen spritzen. • 15-18 Minuten backen.

Christmas Stars with Almond Meringue

Resting time: 1 hour • **Baking time:** 15-18 minutes • **Temperature:** 170°C

Ingredients • For the Christmas Stars • 500 g flour • 250 g softened butter • 6 egg yolk • 125 g sugar

For the meringue • 3 egg whites • 125 g sugar • 125 g ground almonds

Preparation

• Whisk together the butter and sugar until creamy. • Add in the egg yolk and then fold in the sifted flour. Knead the mixture until it forms a smooth dough. • Shape the dough into a ball, cover in cling film and leave to rest for 1 hour in a cool place. • Roll out the dough until it is 4 mm thick. • Cut out star shapes using a pastry cutter. Place these on the baking paper or silicone sheet and set aside. • Preheat the oven to 150°C.

Meringue • Beat the egg whites until fluffy. When reasonably firm, add in the sugar and continue beating until stiff. • Gently fold in the ground almonds with a spatula. • Using a piping bag, place a nut-sized mound of the meringue mixture in the centre of each star. • Bake for 15-18 minutes.

Zitronen- oder Orangennuggets

Ruhezeit: 1 Nacht • *Backzeit:* 30 Minuten • *Temperatur:* 180°

Zutaten • 250 g Mehl • 1 Kaffeelöffel Backpulver • 75 g Zucker • 125 g temperierte Butter • 1 Ei • Füllung • 125 g gemahlene Mandeln oder Haselnüsse • 150 g Zucker • geriebene Schale und Saft von einer Zitrone oder Orange • Glasur • 125 g Puderzucker • 2 Suppenlöffel Zitronen- oder Orangensaft

Zubereitung

• Mehl, Backpulver und Zucker vermischen. • Danach Ei und temperierte Butter dazu geben und zwischen den Händen reiben und zu einer kompakten Masse zusammen drücken. • Danach den Teig zu einer Kugel formen und eine Nacht im Kühlen ruhen lassen.

Am nächsten Tag • Backofen auf 180° vorheizen.

Füllung richten • Mandeln/Haselnüsse, geriebene Zitronen- oder Orangenschale, Saft und Zucker verrühren. • Jetzt Teig ausrollen und die Hälfte in eine gefettete Backform geben. • Die Füllung auf dem Teig gleichmäßig verteilen. • Danach die zweite Hälfte des Teiges ausrollen und darüber legen. • Mit einer Gabel die obere Teigfläche etwas einstechen. • 30 Minuten bei 180° backen.

Glasur • Zucker, Zitronen-oder Orangensaft zu einer glatten Masse verrühren. • Kuchen nach dem Backen damit bestreichen. • Nach dem Abkühlen nach Belieben in Karrees oder Rechtecke schneiden.

Lemon or Orange Nuggets

Resting time: 1 night • *Baking time:* 30 minutes • *Temperature:* 180°C

Ingredients • 250 g flour • 1 teaspoon baking powder • 75 g sugar • 125 g softened butter • 1 egg • Filling • 125 g ground almonds or hazelnuts • 150 g sugar • The grated rind and juice of one lemon or orange • Glaze • 125 g icing sugar • 2 tablespoons lemon or orange juice

Preparation

• Mix together the flour, baking powder and sugar. • Add in the egg and softened butter and rub the mixture together with your fingers until it forms a compact dough. • Shape the dough into a ball and leave overnight to rest in a cool place.

The following day • Preheat the oven to 180°C.

Make the filling • Stir together the almonds/hazelnuts, grated lemon or orange peel, juice and sugar. • Roll out half the dough and place in a greased baking tin. • Spread the filling evenly over the pastry. • Roll out the remaining dough and lay over the filling. • Prick out the top layer of dough with a fork. • Bake for 30 minutes at 180°C.

Glaze • Stir the sugar and lemon or orange juice until smooth. Brush the mixture over the baked pastry. • Once cool, cut the pastry into squares or rectangles, according to preference.

Textes et recettes

Nicole BURCKEL, Bernardette HECKMANN

et les Boulangers d'Alsace

Photographies

Frédérique CLÉMENT

(Pages 5, 11, 15, 17, 19, 21, 23, 27, 29, 31, 33, 35, 39, 41, 43, 47, 49,
53, 55, 57, 59, 61, 63)

I.D. l'Édition

9, rue des Artisans - 67210 Bernardswiller
Tél. 03 88 34 22 00 - Fax : 03 88 34 26 26
info@id-edition.com - www.id-edition.com

ISBN : 978-2-36701-085-4
Imprimé en UE - septembre 2016